i llarsThatPowe rDe stiny
© 2018 Abraham A. Adeyemo (+2348037206951)

ISBN: 978-978-56475-0-1

Unless otherwise stated, all scriptures are taken from the
New King James version of the Holy Bible
(c) 1982 by Thomas Nelson, Inc.

Published by
Power House Publications
Lifeline Tabernacle
Destiny Place: 1-3 Lifeline Avenue
High Court Bus Stop, Ring Road
P.O. Box 41049, Ibadan, Oyo State, Nigeria

www.lifelinetabernacle.org

Cover design: Whitefield Books 08131513534

Printers: ATR Communications 08033593739

Contents

INTRODUCTION

PILLARS form important part of every physical structure. They serve as essential part that provide support and give shape and strength to the structure whether buildings or bridges. For superstructures particularly, pillars form a firm and upright support. We can liken a physical structure to the destiny of every living soul. We are described in the scriptures as God's building:

> *For we are God's fellow workers; you are God's field, you are God's building.*1 Corinthians 3:9.

As God's building therefore, there necessarily has to be pillars that serve as support for our total destiny. If we take the Almighty as the Architect, the Engineer and the wise Masterbuilder, then, it is appropriate to liken human life to physical buildings that require a plan (both architectural and structural). It is the plan that will determine the materials for constructing the pillars. For the destiny of man, there is only one single material God puts in use which He recommends for building our life:

> *Get wisdom! Get understanding! Do not forget, nor turn away from the words of my mouth.* Proverbs 4:5.

> *For the LORD gives wisdom; from his mouth come knowledge and understanding.* Proverbs 2:6.

Wisdom is:
> ➢ The application of what we know to build our entire destiny.
> ➢ The last step in thinking process, after which action follows.
> ➢ Locating God's way of doing things; standing on God's style, approach and method, to get answers to questions and solutions to problems.
> ➢ The 'working out' of what we know by faith that God has worked into us.
> ➢ Doing what God tells us to do in order to witness what He has done for us. It is what it takes to possess what heaven has sent across to us.

Wisdom is unlike faith that comes from hearing the Word of God. It does not come to you; you have to **get** it, **look** for it, **seek** for it, **cry** for it, and **pursue** it more than you do for whatever you consider precious and of great value. It is always available but must be sought for directly from God or through wise people that He brings our way.

The wisdom needed to build your destiny according to God's plans and purpose can be found in the Word of God:

> *For we are God's masterpiece. He has created us anew in Christ Jesus, so we can do the good things he planned for us long ago.* Ephesians 2:10 (NLT).

Before you were born, God gave you a unique mixture of spiritual gifts, passions, abilities, personality, and potentials. There is no one like you in the entire universe; no one possesses your unique mix of talents. This is the reason for the uniqueness of your destiny. It is your destiny, not another's. *It's your destiny!* The danger there is that, though it is yours, it is possible to miss it! It has happened and still happening to several. In fact, it is possible to go through life and miss out on God's purpose ~ by choices. Anyone who chooses to chase every other thing in life other than God and what He has revealed will miss it in very tragic sense.

You can know God's will for your life and seek it to its fulfillment. Even when you face serious challenges, God can turn disaster into destiny. It's never too late to have His perfect will prevail in your life which is the reason this book, *Pillars that Power Destiny* is put together. This book takes you through three symbolic Pillars: *Discovery*, *Desire*, and *Decision*, as necessary for building a lasting and enviable destiny. No matter where you have been or where you are, the Wise Masterbuilder of Destiny - the Lord Jesus Christ - will get you in line with His purpose and establish you in your life assignment. He wants you to fulfill your destiny more than you do! Be blessed as you read.

DESTINY *Defined*

NO LIFE on earth is an accident. Every living soul has a destiny ~ something *to do in this life, exclusive* ~ that only such a person can accomplish. God knows everything that will happen in our lives, and He has scheduled our days to represent the totality of our destiny. The life we now live is preparatory for the next. God wants us to practice on earth what we will do forever in eternity. God has every life planned from the cradle to the grave.

> *Like an open book, you watched me grow from conception to birth; all the stages of my life were spread out before you, The days of my life all prepared before I'd even lived one day.* Psalms 139:16 (MSG).

> *All the days planned for me were written in your book before I was one day old.* Psalm 139:16 (NCV).

Destiny is regarded as the totality of the life of an individual on planet earth. It is the summation of several destinations in the journey of life. Just as no one has the power to determine how one came into the world, so also the destiny of every living soul is predetermined by God who has a purpose for every of His creation. Destiny can therefore be defined as:

> **Predetermined or pre-ordained course of events considered as something beyond human power or control.**

Before we were born, God has wired us with certain ambitions, desires, and drives to play particular roles in history – one that only every one of us as individuals can play. We have the opening chapter of the Book of Jeremiah giving us a clue about divine preparation for every soul brought into the world:

> *Then the word of the Lord came to me, saying: before I formed you in the womb I knew you; before you were born I sanctified you; I ordained you a prophet to the nations.* Jeremiah 1:4,5.

This means we all have a pre-set destiny which has to do with God's purpose and our life assignment. It reveals that destiny is not determined by the intention or preparation of parents no matter how well organized or concerned they were before their new baby arrived.

It further clears the air about the unimportance of the psychological state of the mother whose womb carries the baby to the point of delivery. It means a baby born by a mentally imbalanced mother will not necessarily have a defective or traumatized destiny. The womb therefore serves only as a passage to birth the baby into his or her destiny and not as a prison to determine such life. It further shows also that each person's destiny defers from another.

DESTINY *versus* FATE

We must not confuse destiny with fate. Fate is usually thought of as a predetermined course of events beyond human control. A typical response to a belief in fate is resignation ~ if we can't change destiny, then why even try? Whatever happens "happens", and we can't do anything about it. This is called "fatalism," and it is not biblical. Fatalism is a supernatural belief, and it can indeed have harmful consequences for the way we act in the world. Believing that whatever happens is predestined and inevitable can undermine personal responsibility and lead to paralysis. Fate is antithetical to faith as belief in it has no object or basis. Fate is taken as the development of events beyond a person's control, regarded as determined by a supernatural power. Destiny on the other hand has to do with divinely set events that will necessarily happen to a particular person or thing in the future.

COMMON DESTINY

The destiny of every human being can be captured in the primary purpose of God for creating man as declared before the first man, Adam was made:

> *And God said, Let us make man in our image, after our likeness: and let them have dominion over the fish of the sea, and over the fowl of the air, and over the cattle, and over all the earth, and over every creeping thing that creepeth upon the earth.* Genesis 1:26.

The destiny of man primarily is to be like God and live in dominion. The mind of God was to have a natural or visible likeness of Him on the earth – a person with a physical body – who will rule on the earth as He does in heaven. God breathed into the dust of the ground and formed man He could relate with on the earth as He does as a spirit with the angels in heaven.

> *The heaven, even the heavens, are the LORD'S: but the earth hath he given to the children of men.* Psalm 115:16.

The destiny of man was for humans to be like God in his personality and rule like God on the earth in dominion. Man was made in the nature of God – the divine nature – and empowered to express that nature in dominion. Man became the visible expression of the invisible God on planet earth. It was humanity "carrying" divinity on the earth!

The dominion status of man is an empowerment, a "wiring", an "engineering", an equipping, a programming, and an enablement to be in control; to govern, to rule and exercise authority on the earth. It is a pre-set arrangement of God for man. It is a divine design for what God would assign man to do. It was after this God took man to the place where he would live his destiny; a place He prepared for him. Destiny is about divine preparation that powers a man to live his purpose and accomplish his assignment on earth.

Destiny is about the making of a person and the positioning of same where it is prepared for such. Adam was taken to where his dominion status would have full expression:

> *And the LORD God took the man, and put him into the Garden of Eden to dress it and to keep it.* Genesis 2:15.

The common destiny of man took a new turn when Adam got deceived through Eve, the wife, and this led to their expulsion form the Garden of Eden. The fall of man brought about a slight change to his divine destiny. Both the divine *nature* he carried and the dominion *status* were badly and unalterably damaged by sin. God had to put into force the plan of redemption that had been there before creation. Man had to be redeemed from his sin and restored to his predestined position:

> *What is man, that You are mindful of him, And the son of man, that You visit him? For You have made him a little lower than the angels, And have crowned him with glory and honour. You have made him to have dominion over the works of Your hands; You hast put all things under his feet.* Psalm 8:4-6.

Through redemption, our Lord Jesus, the Son of God, took the sin of mankind to the Cross and paid the penalty for death. He was crucified to remove the curse placed on Adam and was raised from the dead to make us right in the sight of His Father who becomes ours too when we put our faith in all He did for us.

BELIEVERS' COMMON DESTINY

Redemption through Christ re-defined God's relationship with mankind. Two things redemption clearly revealed:

1. The image of God that He wanted man to be like. It was our Lord Jesus Christ, the Son of God that mirrored that image. His coming gave clarity to who the Father is in the spirit. He became the God that man could not see.

   No one has ever seen God. The only Son,
   who is the same as God and is at the
   Father's side, he has made him known.
   John 1:18 (GNB).

2. The love that God had always had for mankind was fully expressed through the sacrifice of Christ on the cross.

The love of God became the new basis for every dealing God would have with man. His love "extended" Him from being the God of all creation to being the Father of those that put their faith in His Son, our Lord, Jesus Christ. A new covenant changed His relationship with mankind with a promise to those who believe in Christ:

> *...As God has said: I will dwell in them, and walk in them; I will be their God, and they shall be my people. Therefore come out from among them, and be separate, says the Lord, do not touch what is unclean, and I will receive you. I will be a Father to you, and you shall be my sons and daughters, says the Lord Almighty.* 2Corinthians 6:16-18.

It was this promise in the new covenant that redefined the destiny of man. God's relationship with man changed from all-inclusive dealing that was aborted by Adam to "exclusive" people who acknowledge they are sinners and accept the offer of His Son, Jesus for the forgiveness of their sins. Though God's love is to every soul He brings into the world, His divine nature and dominion status granted at the beginning are for only those who welcome His offer of grace.

Grace is the major determinant of believers' destiny. We serve a God of plan, purpose, intention and objectivity. Whatever we experience with Him is part of His overall plan and purpose which had been ever before creation. The summary of our destiny as saints are as found in the Scriptures:

> *For whom He foreknew, He also predestined to be conformed to the image of His Son, that He might be the firstborn among many brethren. Moreover whom He predestined, these he also called; whom He called, these He also justified; whom and He justified, these He also glorified.* Romans 8:29, 30 (NKJV).

The five works of grace are as follows:-

1.   **We Are Chosen.**
      Our Christian life does not start at the point of salvation. God had always known from the beginning what He would with us. Being bona-fide children of God commenced when we were in the mind of the Father. He had known us before we knew He did. He chose us before we were conceived in the womb.

*Just as He chose us in Him before the
foundation of the world, that we should
be holy and without blame before Him
in love.* Ephesians 1:4.

*For we are God's masterpiece. He has
created us anew in Christ Jesus, so we
can do the good things he planned for us
long ago.* Ephesians 2:10 (NLT).

2.   **We Are Set Apart.**
        He sets our destiny apart to be like His Son,
        Jesus. He decided from the outset to shape
        our lives along the same lines as the life of
        his Son. He appointed us to have the same
        form as the image of his Son. Therefore,
        God *foreordained our lives from the beginning*
        to be moulded into the image of His Son in
        order for Him to become the firstborn
        among many brethren.

        *For He foreordained us (destined us,
        planned in love for us) to be adopted
        (revealed) as His own children through
        Jesus Christ, in accordance with the
        purpose of His will [because it pleased
        Him and was His kind intent]*
        Ephesians 1:5 (AMP).

We can conclude that the unchanging plan of God has always been to adopt into His own family as many people will receive His Son as their personal Lord and Saviour. He fulfilled this plan by sending Christ to die for them.

3.   **We Are Called.**
He calls us to Himself. His calling is the revelation of His love for us. God calls people by name to draw them to Himself. He does this because of our fallen nature that has distanced us from Him. This makes it impossible for any sinful soul to approach God except such is called. It is the hand of grace that draws us to the throne for salvation and blessing.

No one can come to Me unless the Father who sent me draws him; and I will raise him up at the last day. John 6:44.

4.   **We Are Declared Not Guilty.**
He justifies us. He forgives and acquits us of our sin and puts us into right standing with Himself. He regards the sacrifice of His Son as sufficient to clear us of every unrighteousness. With this acquittal, we have access to the Father ~ this is the crux of the New Covenant.

> *For I will be merciful to their*
> *unrighteousness, and their sins and*
> *lawless deeds I will remember no more.*
> Hebrews 8:12.

5.   **We Are Glorified.**
      He glorifies us. He shares with us the power
      by which He rules in heaven. He empowers
      us for dominion by putting us in charge on
      the earth as He is in heaven. He *raises us to a*
      heavenly dignity and condition or state of being.
      He does what he did in His Son when he
      came as the Word of God.

> *And the Word became flesh and dwelt*
> *among us, and we beheld His glory, the*
> *glory as of the only begotten of the Father,*
> *full of grace and truth.* John 1:14.

Jesus Christ, who is the Word, gave us His life on
the Cross to assure us that, He in us, is like we in
Him, living in dominion. This is the destiny of
every child of God.

WHAT CONSTITUTES PERSONAL DESTINY ?

The sum total of a person's destiny is who the
person will be and what the person will live to do –

the life assignment of the person. It aligns with the purpose from the beginning – to be like Christ and to live like Christ within the assignment God has designed such for.

We can take a cue from our Lord Jesus Christ. Before He was born, an angel of the Lord outlined his destiny to Joseph.

> *And she will bring forth a Son, and you shall call His name JESUS, for He will save His people from their sins.* Matthew 1:21.

His name indicated He will be a Saviour which correlates with His life assignment – to save people from their sins. It was not a personal name the Father gave the Son; it was a functional identity that relates to His life purpose. It was a descriptive reference to what he was to be born to live for.

The forerunner of Christ carried the same functional identity that related to his personal destiny. When asked by the Priests and Levites sent by the religious elders about who he was,

> *He said: I am the voice of one crying in the wilderness, make straight the way of*

the Lord," as the prophet Isaiah said.
John 1:23.

He knew they were least bothered about his personal name. They wanted to know who he was born to be and for what he was born.

The story of Samson presents a different scenario. Before he was born his parents had an encounter with an angel of the Lord, and after his birth was foretold, his father asked a fundamental question that had to do with the unborn child's destiny:

> *Manoah said, Now let your words come to pass! What will be the boy's rule of life, and his work?* Judges 13:12.

Samson's father was curious about the destiny of a child that has not even been conceived in the womb!

DISCOVERY

A DESTINY that will be fulfilled must start from discovery and not decisions. Though decisions determine destiny, but discovery is the starting point. It is not about who or where one wants to be in life because no one decided to come into this world on his or her own. There is no one who came into this world through a choice of time of birth, parents, location, tribe or nation. Man comes by divine initiative based on His plans, purpose and agenda.

Discovery is a journey you have to personally undertake. It is not a one-time exercise. God would not unfold the details of your entire destiny in one encounter. You have to set your heart to constantly seek to catch a picture of your future. This will come through diligent study of the Word of God, constant fellowship with God in prayer and praise, and relationship with those God will bring across as helpers of your destiny.

It is wonderful to note that God earnestly desires to reveal our destiny to us. He never planned that we would live Christ's life without direction, guidance and instruction. He gave us the Holy Spirit for this purpose – to make known to us who He has made us to be and what he has put in us to fulfill our life assignment and accomplish His purpose here on earth. Interestingly, the two profound prayers from Paul the apostle for the Church are aimed at discovering our destiny in Christ:

> *I pray that your hearts will be flooded with light that you will see something of the future he has called you to share.* Ephesians 1:18 (TLB).

> *So ever since we first heard about you we have kept on praying and asking God to help you understand what he wants you to do; asking him to make you wise about spiritual things.* Colossians 1:9 (TLB).

Discovery of your destiny is your license to enthronement. It will put into your hands the plan and purpose of God for your life. Without this, life becomes frustrating, restless, an experiment, subjective and without direction. Discovery will put you in control of your life and destiny under God. It will establish your identity and future.

Look at these wonderful discoveries and the journey each undertook:

JESUS CHRIST

> *And there was delivered unto him the book of the prophet Esaias. And when he had opened the book, he found the place where it was written. The Spirit of the Lord is upon me, because he hath anointed me to preach the gospel to the poor; he hath sent me to heal the brokenhearted, to preach deliverance to the captives, and recovering of sight to the blind, to set at liberty them that are bruised. To preach the acceptable year of the Lord. Luke 4:17, 18.*

Our Lord, Jesus Christ discovered His destiny from the Word of God and specifically from the prophecy of Isaiah.

JOHN THE BAPTIST

> *In those days came John the Baptist, preaching in the wilderness of Judea, And saying, repent ye: for the kingdom of heaven is at hand. For this is he that was spoken of by the prophet Esaias, saying,*

> *The voice of one crying in the wilderness,*
> *prepare ye the way of the Lord, make His*
> *paths straight.* Matthew 3:1-3.

The forerunner of our Lord discovered His destiny from the Word of God and specifically from the book of Isaiah, the prophet.

DANIEL

> *In the first year of Darius the son of*
> *Ahasuerus, of the seed of the Medes,*
> *which was made king over the realm of the*
> *Chaldeans; In the first year of his reign I*
> *Daniel understood by books the number of*
> *the years, whereof the word of the lord*
> *came to Jeremiah the prophet, that he*
> *would accomplish seventy years in the*
> *desolation of Jerusalem.* Daniel 9:1, 2.

Daniel discovered he was a prophet and deliverer to the nation of Israel from the Word of God and specifically from the prophecy of Jeremiah.

MOSES

> *And when he was full forty years old, it*
> *came into his heart to visit his brethren,*
> *the children of Israel. And seeing one of*

> *them suffer wrong, he defended him, and avenged him that was oppressed, and smote the Egyptian: For he supposed his brethren would have understood how that God by his hand would deliver them: but they understood not.* Acts 7:23-25.

Moses knew through his parent the promise of God for his life that he has been raised as a deliverer to the people of Israel when in bondage in Egypt.

PAUL

> *But when it pleased God, Who separated me from my mother's womb, and called me by his grace, to reveal his Son in me, that I might preach him among the heathen; immediately I conferred not with flesh and blood.* Galatians 1:15-16.

Paul discovered his purpose for living after a personal encounter with the Lord Jesus on the way to Damascus.

ESTHER

> *For if thou altogether holdest thy peace at this time, then shall there enlargement and deliverance arise to the Jews from*

> *another place; but thou and thy father's house shall be destroyed: and who knoweth whether thou art come to the kingdom for such a time as this?* Esther 4:14.

Queen Esther was able to fulfill her calling through divine connection and counsel of her uncle, Mordecai.

JACOB

> *And He said, Your name shall no longer be called Jacob, but Israel; for you have struggled with God and with men, and have prevailed.* Genesis 30:28.

Jacob discovered his true destiny through a personal struggle with an angel of the Lord. It was in that encounter his original identity as Israel was revealed and it began to reshape his life and destiny.

JOSEPH

The discovery of Joseph's destiny came through two dreams he had. In the first dream, his eleven bothers bowed to his sheaves and in the second dream, both his parents and all his brothers bowed to him. It was these dreams that prepared him to go through all the travails of life knowing fully well there was a destination God was taking him to. The discovery prepared him to recognise opportunities, accepted them as they came in Potiphar's house and in the prison. He maximised them for God's glory. It was Joseph's belief in his dreams that made him recognise the baker and the butler as opportunities for pardon from imprisonment. He treated them more than they deserved and got rewarded when the butler remembered him at the opportune time.

From the cases we have seen, the journey of discovery starts when you catch a vision of your destiny either through the written Word of God, through dreams or through godly relationship. It is your discovery that prepares you to face your future. The future is not about a time to come, it is rather a process to follow. That process begins with gaining insight into the perfect plan of God for your life.

Every great accomplishment begins as a dream in someone's heart. All things are created twice: first in your mind, and then in your life. Dreamers allow their minds to wander outside the boundaries of what is, creating a mental picture of what can be. They are not always the most talented or best educated ~ just the ones who refuse to put brackets around their thinking or limit themselves to what others have done. Remember, it is not the best of the people that get the best but those that make the most of their time and every opportunity.

We live in a dreamers' world and it is dreamers that rule. Anyone who does not have a dream is doomed. It is the person with a dream that has a guaranteed and secure future. What you dream you can dare. Destiny is a race of responsibility. If you don't want to be a liability, accept responsibility. Don't allow circumstances, people, or your background control you. Take control of your own destiny because it is today's discovery that will lead you into decisions which will give form to tomorrow's realities.

Your dream has relevance not only in the natural but much more in the realm of the spirit as God Himself declared concerning the builders at Babel, who with one voice decided to build a tower whose top will reach heaven. When God saw what they had embarked upon, He remarked:

> *Behold, the people is one, and they have all one language; and this they begin to*

do: and now nothing will be restrained
from them, which they have imagined to
do. Genesis 11:6.

It is what you imagine that will emerge. Your
expectation sets the pace for your experience. Your
dream of destiny is the force that will drive you to
accomplishment. Dare to dream again through
your journey of discovery! It is the stuff destiny is
made of.

WHAT TO DISCOVER

1.   Who you are – your purpose, your mission
        on earth, your relevance, what you are here
        to contribute to your world, what you are
        here to multiply, what you are loaded with,
        what you are fitted for, the reason you are
        on planet earth, why you wake up daily, why
        God sustains you, the reason for the
        strength you have, the essence of the gifts
        and talents you have, and the reason for
        your educational achievements.

2.   What gives your life meaning, what fully
        engages you that you will not mind doing it
        free of cost though you will necessarily be
        paid. It is what you feel drawn to every time,

what you do with ease, what you do with joy, what fulfills you, and what adds value to the lives of others.

When you discover the purpose for your existence, living becomes fruitful, fulfilling and rewarding. Discovery of your destiny removes limits from your life.

THE KEYS TO DISCOVERY

You need some relevant keys to unlock the door of your destiny. Discovery does not happen in a flash. There are applicable keys that allow free flow of revelations, flashes of vivid pictures and strong perceptions.

1. **Faith**
    Without faith in God, nothing can be received from Him. You must believe in God as the very and only Source for your life and destiny. He is the architect of every life, the engineer of our circumstances and the builder of destinies.

    For every house is built by someone, but
    He that built all things is God.
    Hebrews 3:4.

As the Builder, He alone knows the kind of "house" he wants to make out of you. He is also the Porter and we all are clays. He fashions us according to the purpose and programme He has for our lives. Like the human porter, he remoulds the destiny of anyone whose life is marred; appearing out of shape and form.

Look, as the clay is in the potter's hand,
so are you in My hand, O house of Israel!
Jeremiah 18:6.

Approach Him by faith for the details of your destiny. Ask Him questions about your life. Ask with confidence. Ask with expectation of response from Him. Ask prayerfully in understanding and in the language of the Spirit. Ask meditatively. Be like the prophet of old, who completely bewildered by the evil of his days sought the Lord for His mind:

I will stand upon my watch, and set me
upon the tower, and will watch to see
what he will say unto me, and what I
shall answer when I am reproved. And
the LORD answered me, and said, write
the vision, and make it plain upon

tables, that he may run that readeth it.
Habakkuk 2:1, 2 (KJV).

2. **Curiosity**

Most of the things we call precious require a prospector. Every prospecting or exploration is preceded by curiosity i.e. a searching mind. Curiosity means being adventurous. It is being inquisitive about the rule of your life. It is a hunger for the facts of your destiny in the mind of your Maker. To get a vision you must look out. Curiosity means living your life outside of the box; not being satisfied with things as they are, but eager to enter into the reality of life as divinely prepared to appear. Curiosity demands high level of sensitivity and alertness.

3. **Understanding**

Understanding must have a place in our lives for us to occupy our rightful place in destiny. You need divine understanding concerning what is being revealed to you as you journey through discovery of your destiny. Assumption should not be allowed. Clarity of every information, sign and instruction is of utmost essence. When Mary was told by the angel, Gabriel that she would give birth to the Son of God, she asked for understanding:

Then Mary said to the angel, How can this be, since I do not know a man? Luke 1:34.

The angel in response told her the exact steps it would take by God to make it happen in her. Understanding gives credence to your discovery and powers you for decision. God knows we need to fully assimilate and accommodate what He is passing across in our minds, so He gives room for inquiry into details if necessary. When Gideon was mandated by the angel to deliver Israel from the oppression of the Midianites, he immediately from the point of his natural weakness started to plead for more light, and this was the understanding he received:

And the Lord said to him, Surely I will be with you, and you shall defeat the Midianites as one man. Judges 6:16.

4.   **Meekness**
It takes a teachable spirit to receive what the Lord has for our destiny. Destiny is not our

ambition, our desires, our plans or the way we think our lives should be. It is God's perfect predestination. It is His decision for our destiny that He wants us to discover and cooperate with Him to live it successfully. You must be willing to learn and unlearn at same time. Gideon had to unlearn his visible weakness and Mary had to "unlearn" her virginity and single status for both to fully grasp what God has planned for them.

Meekness is accepting your human limit to tap into divine un-limitedness. It took the meekness of Moses for God to still reveal his true destiny and calling at the "over ripe" age of eighty years.

5. **Patience**

Destiny is a race we must all run. Discovery is the start point where we must begin to exercise patience. Patience is the ability to endure and persevere in seeking for light concerning the details of your destiny. Destiny is also a promise of God to establish us in His perfect will and enable us live a life that glorifies Him.

That you do not become sluggish, but imitate those who through faith and patience inherit the promises. Hebrews 6:12.

Visions, dreams and revelations from God do not come in torrents but in bits and pieces. He will not show you the whole picture of your destiny from cradle to grave. No! The Lord will make known to you only the bit you can handle at a time; sufficient to take you to your next destination as programmed by Him. It is only those who are teachable at heart and patient in their spirit that will journey through in constant discovery of their destiny.

For precept must be upon precept, precept upon precept, Line upon line, line upon line, Here a little, and there a little. Isaiah 28:10.

CATCHING THE DREAM OF DESTINY

Destiny is like a dream that God gives to actualise His plans and purpose. It is the picture of the future He has set for every individual. It is the details of His future activities in the lives of His people. Soon after God called Abraham, He gave him a vision that revealed the nation that will be birthed through him and what the future of that nation would look like.

When God called Joseph, he gave him a dream twice that clearly depicted the details of his destiny. Without a dream, destiny is doomed. Destiny is a race of responsibility, if you don't want to be a liability, accept responsibility. Your imagination determines your destination. Look beyond where you are so you can arrive where God destined for you. In case you are going through something, it is good to know that it is so for everyone living. It is so because everyone is going somewhere.

What you call problems are simply passages that *leads* you to your purpose, and not prisons that lock people in. It is your dream that takes you into the reality of your future before you get there. Your dream when pursued will most likely predict your future. No dream, no future! Note, God has promised you a future:

> *For I know the thoughts that I think toward you, says the Lord, thoughts of peace, and not of evil, to give you a future and a hope.* Jeremiah 29:11.

That future will be actualized through your dream. Your dream does not have an expiration date. The future belongs to those who believe in the beauty of their dreams.

STEPS TO CATCHING THE DREAM/VISION OF DESTINY

1.   Ask God in Prayer and Study.

It will take asking to receive whatever we want from God. Asking to know what we believe is already there for us is a strong indication of our willingness to cooperate with God concerning the affairs of our life. God needs our willingness and obedience to see the project of our life succeed. He has the blueprint and the details which are there not for His keeping but for revelation to us as and when we are ready for us. He will definitely not impose the destiny He has for us on us.

Through specific and direct prayers for enlightenment concerning our future, we will not only make discovery through hearing God speak, but also through dreams and revelations in vivid pictures. When we hear God, the things we do don't make sense but the proofs will show. Adequate and specific time must be set aside for this kind of prayer because His response would not come hurriedly as for other prayers. There must be readiness to wait on Him for as long as the mystery of His plans would unfold.

Asking God in prayer also means putting the mind on "neutral gear" without any preconceived idea or schemes. It means laying the heart like a page not yet written on. This allows the Spirit of God to write on the heart the same way He did on the tablets of stone provided by Moses on the mountain. Prayer must be made in faith resting on God's promises particularly the one made through Jeremiah, the prophet:

> *Call to Me, and I will answer you, and show great and mighty things, which you do not know.* Jeremiah 33:3.

Study of the Word will also reveal the plans of destiny. Through the Lord Jesus, we learnt that within the written Word is what has been written concerning every one of us. The Bible contains the Word written for living. We are born again to live by the Word. It is the Word that reveals the will of God for our lives. It was within the written Word that the Lord Jesus and His forerunner, John the Baptist, found the direction of their destiny. It is the Word of God that renews our mind to jettison our old ways of life and turn to God to discover our true destiny.

> *And do not be conformed to this world: but be transformed by the renewing of your mind, that you may prove what is that good, and acceptable, and perfect, will of God.* Romans 12:2.

The ministry of the Holy Spirit will help in our prayers and study of The Word. Jesus sent the Spirit of Truth to guide us and lead us into everything that has been prepared for us. The Spirit of God is committed to help us and has been given authority to guide us into our destiny. He is our Helper, Comforter, and Teacher. God's goal is that the Spirit of Truth will would lead us so that He can show us the possible future.

2. Ask Yourself in Introspection

Journey of discovery does not start and end with God, you will need to take a further step and ask yourself who you want to be and what you want to do if everything is available; that is your dream of your destiny. This is what introspection is all about – looking inward, a reflection, the act or process of self-examination, or the inspection of your thoughts and feelings. What you are doing is that you are capturing the mental picture of your future which obviously will correlate with revelations you are getting from God.

Your destiny is where your love and pain intersect. When you feel pain and love for a particular problem or need in society, or for a particular place or people, this may be pointing to your destiny. It is where your passion lies, where your heart quickens, and where you feel an almost supernatural hunger to intervene and improve a situation. Ask yourself these key questions that will help your discovery process:

> - **What do you love and enjoy doing?** Sometimes what we call a hobby is really our calling.
> - **What do you have passion for?** What sets you on fire and consumes you with zeal?
> - **What makes you angry and frustrated?** What problems can you not get out of your head? You may be called to confront those problems with your talent and time.

3. Ask by Observation

Discovery of destiny is a journey that has no defined route because life itself is a mystery that only the Almighty can unravel. God uses several means to awaken what He has put in us even when we are not seeking the knowledge directly from Him or asking from within ourselves.

The story of Muhammad Yunus, founder of Grameen Bank, is a classic example of someone who discovered his true calling from the environment and circumstances he found himself. His story is told in Stephen Covey's book, *The 8th*

Habit. He didn't have any vision to begin with. He simply saw someone in need, tried to fill it, and the vision evolved. Yunus' vision of a poverty-free world was set in motion through extending microcredit to the poorest of the poor in the nation of Bangladesh. He started from granting credit to forty-two people with $27 and graduated to establish a bank with 1,267 branches and over 12,000 staff members lending more than $4.5 billion in loans!

Studying some of the world's great leaders, one would notice that their sense of vision usually evolve slowly; the vision of what is possible suddenly burst upon their consciousness. But generally speaking, visions of destiny comes as people sense human need and respond to their conscience in trying to meet that need. And when they meet that need, they see another, and meet that, and on and on.

When you are inspired by some great purpose, some extraordinary project, all your thoughts break their bounds. Your mind transcends limitations, your consciousness expands in every direction, and you find yourself discovering your true destiny with a strong sense of purpose.

THE POWER OF YOUR DREAM
OVER YOUR AGE

Age has its place but it is limited concerning the fulfillment of God's purpose because God determines the timing of every individual. It is not about how old or how young one is, but how well one has caught the dream or vision of his or her destiny. Your dream and vision of your destiny is bigger than your age because it has a lasting nature. Age is timed, but dreams are timeless. Dreams always outlast the dreamer.

> *I said, Age should speak, and multitude of years should teach wisdom, but there is a spirit in man, and the breath of the Almighty gives him understanding.* Job 32:8, 9.

Your dream and vision is bigger than your age because it is what separates you from others. It gives you an identity, uniqueness, a sort of branding. Men and women are known by their dreams; men like Abraham, Deborah, Graham Bell, Mother Theresa, Michael Faraday, Isaac Newton, and Martin Luther King, the Wright brothers, Thomas Edison and several other achievers. It is your dream and vision and not your age that takes you into the reality of your future, before you get there. Moses was already eighty years before he encountered his true destiny. Joseph and David were young men when their stars began to shine.

It is also your dream and vision that sets you free from the limitation of what eyes can see. The poorest person is not the one without money, but the one without a dream. Poor eyes limit a man's sight, poor vision or dream limits his deeds. Your dream and vision gives you an unusual sense of responsibility. If you can think of how far a blind man can go without being a burden, that is the kind of burden or liability anyone is who has no dream or vision of his or her life purpose. It is your dream that puts you in the driver seat of your destiny. Without vision life is like a game. Men and women with dreams and visions see father than others. They have empires in their brains!

Our Lord Jesus obviously had information about his birth ~ the encounter of the mother with angel Gabriel, the primary evidence through the testimony of Elizabeth pregnant with John the Baptist, the wise men who came visiting with gifs, the prophecies of Simeon and Anna, and several others that were not written.

The first opportunity He had at age 12 years was to go the temple among the teachers of the law to learn how to go about His mission. At that tender age, He stopped living His age and started living His dream, which was to be about His Father's business (Luke 2:46-52). From that moment, He began to increase in wisdom and stature. When you live your dream and not your age, you increase as well in the knowledge of your calling and life assignment, and you also become an attraction both to God and men.

DANGERS OF LIVING YOUR AGE

1. Living your age will waste you away whereas living your dream will give you a way in your world and make you a way for others.

    A man's gift makes room for him, and brings him before great men. Proverbs 18:16.

2. Living your age will put you in constant agony, under pressure and possible regret of what you think you should have done but didn't; while living your dream will constantly give you a sense of hope which will make your faith produce.

3.   Living your age will put you in the prison of the memory of the past; whereas, living your dream keeps you excitedly expectant of a better tomorrow and allows you the joy of the good of today.

4.   Living your age keeps you with the concern of the present situation; while living your dream makes you realise that it is your imagination of the future that determines your destination. Imagination is the most powerful gift you possess. It is your dream machine. Therefore use it to dream big dreams.

5.   Living your age wears you out physically and emotionally; whereas, living your dream renews your youth as the dream and vision of your future continually unfold before you. Catching the dream and vision of your future helps you to know your life purpose and pursue it.

BENEFITS OF LIVING YOUR DREAM

1.   Living your dream empowers you to take delivery of your destiny. Without a dream,

destiny is doomed. Dreams are the stuff destiny is made of. You cannot live the life God has prepared except you envision it. You have to see it before you experience it.

2. Living your dream connects you with those God has sent you to and those He has sent to you. It shows you the kind of relationships you must develop in order to be distinguished. A man without a dream is a man without a future; totally disconnected with divine arrangements and visitations.

3. Living your dream gives you divine acceleration; you don't need to be hasty or impatient. When you live your dream, God Himself will accelerate all He has promised to do.

> *Then the Lord said to me, you have seen well, for I am ready to perform my word.* Jeremiah 1:12.

4. Living your dream helps you in your choices.

> *Where there is no revelation, the people cast off restraint; but happy is he who keeps the law.* Proverbs 29:18.

Some people are careless about their choices because they have no vision, no dream of their future. Your dream helps you decide what to tolerate, what to put up with without resistance, what to allow without questioning and what to prioritize. The future is either bought or sold by the choices we make today and the choices we make today are influenced by the dream of the future.

5. Living your dream develops in you the power to see the invisible, believe the incredible, and receive the impossible.

DESIRE

IN THE LIGHT of our pre-ordained **destiny**, there are **desires** that God places within us. Once we see our destiny clearly, the sight of it will create the desire to achieve it. We dream because He dreamed first. It is those dormant dreams we seek to unravel in our journey of discovery. People succeed for a thousand different reasons, but the one thing they all have in common is desire. Destiny depends on the strength of desire.

Destiny discovered needs to be desired for it to be fulfilled. It is the burning desire for visions and revelations received that will give a push through life challenges towards achieving goals and aspirations. If failure stops a man from pressing on, you can count on it, he has lost his desire. As long as desire is burning, there is always fuel to keep life going, for desire determines destiny. This is true in every realm of life. Desire is the fire that pushes us higher. The greater the desire to reach a goal, the more likely it is that goal will be reached.

Desires are very important because they point us on a path toward fulfilling our pre-ordained destiny. You are always moving toward fulfilling your desires. You view your desire with the eyes of your heart, your imagination. Your thoughts are often connected to your desires. Your desires can take you closer to God or further away from Him. This is the reason God wants you to express your desires as you gradually discover what you are born for and born with to make a difference to your world. Indeed, you tend to become what you really desire to be. If this be the case, there are few things in life that are more important than that of developing the desires that will dominate and determine the direction and destination of your life.

Desire can also be regarded as the map we have been given to aid us in the discovery of our true destiny in order to find life worth living. We abandon the most important privilege given by God to partner with us in the shaping of our lives when we abandon desire. We leave our hearts by the side of the road and head off in the direction of fitting in, getting by, being productive or what have you. We must listen to desire, look at it carefully, let it guide us to turn to God who had rightly put it in us and guarantees its fulfillment.

> *Delight yourself also in the LORD, and He shall give you the desires of your heart.* Psalm 37:4.

The mystery of desire is that even though we sleep, our desire does not. Desire is the essence of human soul, the secret of our existence. Absolutely nothing of human greatness is ever accomplished without it. Desire fuels our search for the life we prize. Christianity is an invitation to desire. Jesus related to people in a way of continually taking them into their hearts; to their deepest desire:

> *Therefore I say unto you, what things soever ye desire, when ye pray, believe that ye receive them, and ye shall have them.* Mark 11:24 (KJV).

WHAT IS DESIRE?

Desire is the longing for purpose, the hunger for meaning, the drive to be and to become who you are meant to be. It is the drive to fulfill your potential; the inherent drive of every being to thrive. It is the inner longing; known or unknown, of every individual to add his or her unique luster to the gem of creation. Sight and desire are closely connected. Without a fiery desire, we will not have the conviction to believe in our purpose.

Your desire is what you long for, what or whom you long to be with. Your desire is where your heart is. Your desire is your greatest treasure and will be your reward. It is a strong feeling, worthy or unworthy, that impels to the attainment or possession of something that is (in reality or imagination) within reach. Dreams are the product of desire. The starting point of all accomplishment is desire. The fact that you can imagine a certain kind of lifestyle for yourself is a good indicator that you have a desire. A dream is simply a strongly desired goal. Desire is the key to motivation because it develops within us a passion to pursue that which we long for. Your desires, however, must be backed by good decision making.

Deep burning desire drives a team to do in a few minutes what they could not do in hours. The greater the desire to reach a goal, the more likely it is that goal will be reached. Desire is the spring of human action, and if you want to know what men will do, you must know their system of desires.

THE ENEMY OF DESIRE

The enemy of your destiny cannot destroy your purpose or your life assignment, but he can dilute your desire by getting you distracted from it. Distraction is the greatest enemy of desire when you have discovered your destiny. The wisest man in history and a leader ~ Solomon ~ whose gifts and focus once made him the talk of the world lost direction because he was distracted from his calling. He fell from the lofty height of a great desire for God and the nation of Israel to desiring strange women. Distraction is one temptation that will fight your desire but you do not have to fall for it.

There is a destination God is taking you which you are already fully convinced about. You must make up your mind to stay on that path. You must resist, refuse, and reject any alternative the enemy has to offer. Distraction sometimes comes very subtly that you may not recognise it; it is like an offer of something close or similar to what you are aiming at. It comes as side attraction seeking your attention in order to stop you from reaching your goal. Stay focused always. A burning desire for your pre-ordained destiny is the fuel to your creativity, your motivation and your excitement for living. Weak desires bring weak results, just as a small amount of fire makes a small amount of heat.

Goals intensify desire and increase persistence. They also create an undying zeal to sail through the thick and thin of life. Goals ignite a burning desire in people that ultimately leads them to success.

DECISION

DECISION has a major role to play in determining destiny. There is a God-inspired blueprint that has been predestined for each of us. It is up to us to line up with the predetermined will and desire of God, and collaborate with the purposes of God in order to accomplish God's dream, even while life and the enemies of destiny try to choke out this sense of purpose as well as the creativity to accomplish the task. We have to build our lives according to divinely implanted sense of purpose. This will require us to make decisions that will directly give shape and form to our future.

Decision is the ignition key of progress because the instant one makes a solid decision, change will be automatic. It is one thing to have good desires but it is quite another to make a quality decision of getting up and pursuing those desires. Many people falter in this area because they do not want to make a commitment. Making a quality decision enables you to find the power of being committed towards your desires. Nothing ever changes until a man or woman makes a decision. Decision should lead to determination.

Daniel made a decision that was instrumental to his monumental rise in Babylon. It is decision that determines destiny. You have to always make your own decisions no matter how unimportant. You can take counsel, take advice, listen to direction and guidance but make your own decision that will lead you to take a right action. Refuse to surrender the driver seat of your destiny. You have what it takes to know what to do next. Be very careful of making decisions based upon your personality profile, etc. God is not bound by the way we're "wired." God never dialogues with anybody about how they're wired before he calls them to a job. Consider Moses and quit camouflaging doubt with psychobabble.

LINES TO BE CROSSED

Decisions that will positively impact our destiny must recognise and take proper cognizance of barriers and limitations which represent lines to be crossed. Destiny in a way is a race into which we are born. Everyone born into this world is born to run; no one is exempted. While some are conscious of this fact, there are several others that are not. From the day you were born, you were born into a race. Your birth registered you into a race.

> *Do you not know that those who run in a*
> *race all run, but one receives the prize?*
> *Run in such a way that you may obtain.*
> 1 Corinthians 9:24.

Just like in athletic race where there are specific lines that need to be crossed before you get to the finish line, so also with the race of destiny. There are lines that are normal crossroads or landmarks, imaginary lines and satanic lines, limitations designed along our path to remind us that it will take the grace of God for us to get to our destination. Also there are lines that represent barriers to progress, limitations to motion, oppositions in your way to fulfilling God's purpose, lids placed on your showing forth, veils used to cover your vision, or obstacles on the paths to where God has prepared for you.

Lines also are like seasons or phases of your destiny that you must necessarily journey through for you to arrive at your final destination.

To everything there is a season, a time to every purpose under heaven. Ecclesiastes 3:1.

Whatever season you find yourself in life, God must have timed it for a purpose so you can reap the benefits of it. Joseph was a case in point who went through five phases – from his parents to the pit to Potiphar to Prison and finally to the palace. In each of these phases, God was with him and made him to prosper.

MAJOR LINES TO BE CROSSED

Once you pursue destiny instead of default, you will be resisted by various circumstances and reactions from men. We need a sense of destiny to allow us grow and mature in grace and mercy, simply because life itself and Satan will challenge our destiny. The book of Hebrews in the Bible has a chapter known not just for heroes of faith but for line crossers starting from Abel. There are two line crossers that stand out of them all; Abraham who is the father of faith and Moses who is the prophet of faith.

Using the achievements of these patriarchs, we can identify three of the major lines that must be crossed in order to fulfill destiny.

1.   **The Line of The Unknown**

> *By faith Abraham obeyed when he was*
> *called to go out to the place which he*
> *would receive as an inheritance. And he*
> *went out, not knowing where he was*
> *going.* Hebrews 11:8.

To pursue your vision, fulfill your God-given purpose, and be a person of destiny, you have to cross the line of the unknown. You have to go to places you have never been and meet people you had never met. The two major things that determine your destiny are the places you go and the people you meet. If you have to experience something you have never experienced before, you have to do something you have never done before.

Now, there will be the fear of "What's out here?" "What if I fail?" Nonetheless, you have to be willing to step out into deep waters. That's what makes it a challenge. That's also why the company of the successful is not too crowded.

If you expect to go places you had never been and do things you had never done (in your business, relationship or any pursuit) you have to trust God like Abraham did:

> *Abraham didn't focus on his own impotence and say, It's hopeless. This hundred-year-old body could never father a child. Nor did he survey Sarah's decades of infertility and give up. He didn't tiptoe around God's promise asking cautiously skeptical questions. He plunged into the promise and came up strong, ready for God, sure that God would make good on what he had said.* Romans 4:19-21 (MSG).

You will learn that when you have nothing left but God, you will find out that He is more than enough.

2.   **The Line of the Impossible**

> *By faith Abraham, when he was tested, offered up Isaac: and he who had received the promises offered up his only begotten son, of whom it was said, "In Isaac your seed shall be called,"* *concluding that God was able to raise him up, even from the dead; from which he also received him in a figurative sense.* Hebrews 11:17-19.

Abraham did not only cross the line of the unknown, he also crossed the line of the impossible. He did things that appeared humanly impossible so to say because he had become a person of destiny through his vision of Isaac being after death! This clearly validates the enviable placement of Abraham as the father of faith. It shows that faith is not trying to believe in spite of evidence; it is daring to take steps in spite of the consequence. The impossible is simply the unexplored, unreached, uncharted territory of life like the present United States of America that was discovered by Christopher Columbus when looking for a route to India!

Believing in Christ and obeying God means doing what you cannot do naturally. It is attempting the impossible and performing it like Elijah did on Mt. Carmel when he called down the fire of God. It is running towards your desire or the opposition with a heart established in faith as David did against Goliath. If your goal does not have "Goliath" size, or much bigger than you, you really do not need faith; your common sense will do.

3.   **The Line of The Pull of The World.**
By faith Moses, when he became of age, refused to be called the son of Pharaoh's daughter; choosing rather to suffer affliction with the people of God, than to enjoy the passing pleasures of sin for a season; esteeming the reproach of Christ

> *greater riches than the treasures in Egypt; for he looked to the reward.* Hebrews 11:24-26.

There will be the pull of the world the moment you are set to pursue your purpose and fulfill your destiny. You have to cross the line by making a choice between every passing pleasure that lasts just for a time and the pleasure of God that lasts for eternity. You have to forsake the worldly system, traditions and values and put your hope in God.

There will be a tendency to go back, but the longer you stay across that line, the less the pull you will feel on your soul. Remember how the whole nation of Israel (numbering around three million!) wandered for 40 years because of the unbelief of just ten people. Only two of them, Joshua and Caleb, crossed the line and made it to the Promised Land.

THE MASTER LINE CROSSER

Our Lord Jesus Christ crossed many lines to accomplish His life assignment as the Saviour of mankind. He made a decision by putting Himself under an obligation and thereby overcame every barrier as they presented themselves. He crossed every line with the word, "I MUST".

> *And He said to them, why did you seek Me? Did you not know that* <u>I MUST</u> *be about My Father's business? Luke 2:49. (Emphasis by author).*

> *But He said to them,* <u>I MUST</u> *preach the kingdom of God to the other cities, because for this purpose I have been sent. Luke 4:43. (Emphasis by author).*

> *The Son of Man* <u>MUST</u> *suffer many things, and be rejected by the elders, and chief priests and scribes, and be killed, and be raised on the third day. Luke 9:22 (Emphasis by author).*

> *Nevertheless,* <u>I MUST</u> *journey today and tomorrow, and the day following; for it cannot be that a prophet should perish outside Jerusalem. Luke 13:33. (Emphasis by author).*

> <u>I MUST</u> *work the works of Him who sent Me while it is day; the night is coming when no one can work. John 9:4. (Emphasis by author).*

To cross every line to the fulfilling of your destiny, you have to allow the Holy Spirit move you to make same decision by the reason of Christ's life in you; and put your life under a "MUST" mandate that will take you across every barrier and propel you forward for progress and accomplishment.

DESTINY *Fulfilled*

YOU cannot fulfill your destiny on a theory; it takes work. None of the secrets of success will work unless you do. You are made for action. Success simply takes good ideas and puts them to work. Free enterprise means the more enterprising you are, the more free you are.

Three major factors will contribute to the fulfilling of destiny:

1. Determination
2. Discipline
3. Diligence

DETERMINATION

Determination is the outward evidence of desire and decision and shows in your action. When we determine to pursue what we see, only then will our determination **link up** with God's predetermination, and He will **impart** a supernatural force to help us live in what He has already finished. The race of life is not to the swift but to those who keep on running with the determination never to stop until they win. Determination is the runner that gets up each day and trains. Determination is what the child has as she climbs back on her bicycle without the training wheels for the hundredth time, trying so hard to learn to ride without them. It is determination that sets us apart from others.

Our goals are accomplished through constant determination. *First,* we must know what those goals are. *Second,* we must have a plan and be willing to carry that plan out to meet those goals. This often requires discipline and our will to make it happen no matter what. It is a choice we make. This choice sets us apart from so many others who would rather just settle for a life of mediocrity. Fulfillment of destiny requires an everyday intentional decisions to make something happen and to be willing to carry it out.

Determination is anchored in one's beliefs, values and principles. In many instances, it is based upon one's level of personal faith. Whatever the reason, determination and resoluteness is what allows us to remain motivated and to overcome whatever adversity, obstacles and barriers we may encounter. In order to make Joshua, the young man that took over from Moses after his demise, God had to repeatedly instruct him to be determined:

> *Be strong and of good courage, for to this*
> *people you shall divide as an inheritance*
> *the land which I swore to their fathers to*
> *give them.* Joshua 1:6.

In recent studies of history greatest leaders, there were several traits that were found to be common to most of them, that is, "dynamic determination." This trait relates to the will and speaks of a leader's ability to initiate and establish momentum; to break free from the lethargy that often keeps others from getting started. There is courage and boldness to act and tenacity to sustain the initiative.

Great people don't give up, they live up to the challenges that life throws at them. Great people don't *go* through; they *grow* through the difficulties that come on their path. They start all over again with great hope, with great determination, with great grit, and that is why they reach the highest peak of success that most people only aspire for. They have the fact that: *no challenges, no success, know challenges know success.*

DISCIPLINE

Discipline is what keeps you in the race of life and allows for the fulfillment of your destiny. It is what you must do always to keep in the race. You regard your destiny for what it is really; a race. In a race you dare not look back. A race is a contest of speed. It is time-tagged – time to start and time to finish. It is not any time because there is no time like that. A race is run for one singular purpose – to win a prize. In order to win a prize, there is a price or prices to pay. Discipline is the price to pay for destiny to be fulfilled. Discipline has to do with taking full responsibility for your life.

THE PLACE OF RESPONSIBILITY

Fulfillment of destiny has to do with taking responsibility. There is only one person responsible for the quality of the life you live – that person is you. To be successful, you have to take 100% responsibility for everything you experience in your life. Destiny fulfilled has a lot to do with the level of your achievements, the results you produce, the quality of your relationships. It even goes much farther to be interpreted with the state of your health and physical fitness, your income, your debts, your feelings – everything!

Taking 100% responsibility for your life and destiny means you personally and constantly acknowledge that you create everything that happens to you. It means you understand that you are the cause of all of your experiences. George Washington Carver said, "Ninety-nine of all failures come from people who have a habit of making excuses." If indeed you really want to create the life of your dreams, then you are going to have to take 100% responsibility for your life as well. It means giving up all your excuses, all your victim stories, all the reasons why you can't and why you haven't up till now, and any possibility of blaming of outside circumstances.

Know that if you cannot change the circumstances, the seasons, or the wind, you can change yourself. The day you change your responses is the day your life will begin to get better! Be in control of the thoughts you think, the images you visualize, what you see in your mind and the actions you take. They all determine everything you experience. If you want something different, you are going to have to do something different. You have to take the position that you have always had the power to make it different, to get it right; to produce the desired results.

It is responsibility to constantly find out what it takes to get to where next. When a person refuses to take responsibility; he becomes a liability like a baby. Babyhood is immaturity and the Scripture has a word for it:

> *Woe to you, O land, when your king is a child, and your princes feast in the morning! Blessed are you, O land, when your king is the son of nobles, and your princes feast at the proper time – for strength and not for drunkenness!* Ecclesiastes 10:16, 17.

Comparing "babies" who are immature and grown-ups who are regarded as responsible:

- ➤ Babies cry for their season to come, grown-ups qualify for their season.
- ➤ Babies look for who will employ them, grown-ups deploy their gifts and talents. They know they have something to offer, so they don't suffer.
- ➤ Babies complain about where they are, grown-ups are concerned about where

they are going. They know where they are presently are just passages not prisons.

DILIGENCE

Diligence is simply business-like approach to issues of life and destiny. It is constant and earnest effort to accomplish what is undertaken; persistent exertion of body or mind. It is hard work. It is working hard at the task at hand. Whatever we do should be done deliberately, and effectively. To be idle is to subscribe to poverty. Every word synonymous to blessing is diligence. Slack is synonymous with lack. The sluggish will always end up as rubbish. Those who are slothful always miss their slot in life.

> *He who has a slack hand becomes poor,*
> *but the hand of the diligent makes rich.*
> Proverbs 10:4.

Work your mind to make your life produce for you. It is not just doing something right, but also doing something thoroughly and effectively. Diligence delivers excellence, quality, creativity, and the highest standards possible. Hard work saves from hardship. You must believe in effectiveness and efficiency; not just doing things right but doing the right things at the right time.

The Father's business is to see you finish your course with joy. Have value for your time which is one precious gift God gave every soul equally. Make the most of every opportunity. It is your sense of value concerning your life and destiny that will determine the flow of the grace of God in your direction. This enough can bring about many open doors to your life.

> *Seest thou a man diligent in his business? He shall stand before kings; he shall not stand before mean men.* Proverbs 22:29 (KJV).

Whatever you handle; your job, business, career or your home, do it with your entire mind. You are not destined for failure. Hard work does not kill, it is idleness that destroys a man's destiny gradually. You must move forward! You must make progress! Like a wise man said, "If you cannot fly, run. If you cannot run, walk. If you cannot walk, crawl. Just do something!" If anyone has excuses for doing nothing then such a person should hear this:

> *Take a lesson from the ants, you lazy fellow. Learn from their ways and be wise! For though they had no king to make them work, yet they labour hard all summer, gathering food for the winter.* Proverbs 6:6-9 (TLB).

Great lesson indeed if you humble yourself to learn from their unusual diligence.

THE WISDOM TO BUILD DESTINY

The foundation needed to build destiny through the pillars of discovery, desire and decision is wisdom; the wisdom of God. It is wisdom that builds.

> *Any enterprise is built by wise planning, becomes strong through common sense, and profits wonderfully by keeping abreast of the facts.* Proverbs 24:3, 4. (TLB).

Wisdom that builds comes primarily through learning. It is the reason the Lord Jesus invites us to come and learn of Him (Matthew 16:29) because in Him is all wisdom and knowledge (Colossians 2:3) to live the kind of life He wants us to live.

We invite you to
an encounter with destiny

@

Lifeline Tabernacle
DESTINY PLACE

An assembly of people carrying the life of God and ordained to experience the glory of God arise upon their lives

NATIONAL HEADQUARTERS

Destiny Place: 1-3, Lifeline Avenue,
High Court Bus Stop, Ring Road, Ibadan

LAGOS BRANCH

Destiny House: 10, Taiwo Odekunle Street,
Ifako-Ogba, Lagos